BRET "HITMAN" HART

THE BEST THERE IS, THE BEST THERE WAS, THE BEST THERE EVER WILL BE.

BRET HART WITH PERRY LEFKO

Bret "Hitman" Hart – The Best There Is, The Best There Was, The Best There Ever Will Be

Copyright ©2000 Balmur Book Publishing/Balmur Entertainment Ltd.

Co-Published in ©2000 by:
Balmur Book Publishing
 A Division of Balmur Entertainment Ltd.
35 Alvin Avenue
Toronto, Ontario, M4T 2A7

Stoddart Publishing Co. Limited
34 Lesmill Road
Toronto, Ontario, M3B 2T6

Distributed in Canada by:
General Distribution Services Ltd.,
325 Humber College Blvd.,
Toronto, Ontario, M9W 7C3
Tel. (416)213-1919
Fax (416) 213-1917
Email: customer.service@ccmailgw.genpub.com
        cservice@genpub.com

Distributed in the United States by:
General Distribution Services Inc.,
4500 Witmer Industrial Estates
Niagara Falls, New York, 14305-1386
Toll-free Tel. 1-800-805-1083
Toll-free Fax 1-800-481-6207
Email: gdsinc@genpub.com

Canadian Cataloguing in Publication Data
Hart, Bret ; Lefko, Perry
Bret "Hitman" Hart; The Best There Is, The Best There Was,
The Best There Ever Will Be

ISBN 0-7737-60954

1. Hart Bret 2 . Wrestlers – Canada – Biography. I. Lefko, Perry. II. Title

GV1196.H37A32000 796.812/092 C99-932674-0

U.S. Cataloguing in Publication Data (Library of Congress Standards)

Hart, Bret
    Bret "Hitman" Hart: The best there is, the best there was, the best there ever will be / Bret Hart with Perry Lefko—1st ed.
[ ]p. : col. ill. ; cm.
Includes bibliographic references and index.
Summary: A biography of the professional wrestler, from a well know wrestling family in Canada, who has won both the World Wrestling Federation and World Championship Wrestling titles.
ISBN 0-7737-6095-4

1. Hart Bret 2 . Wrestlers – Canada – Biography. I. Lefko, Perry. II. Title

769.812/092 [B] 21   2000 CIP

Cover Design: Dave Murphy/ArtPlus Design & Communications
Page Layout: Barb Neri & Carlos Reyes/ArtPlus Design & Communications
Printed and bound in Canada

Acknowledgments

The hardest part about trying to thank everyone that has helped me get this far is the fear of leaving someone out. I'll try my best not to do that.

I want to first thank my late brother, Dean, who defined me as a character and taught me to never quit as I grew up. My best friends as a kid: Dean Wilkinson, Mike Bracko and Jim Cummings – who are still my best friends. Thank you for keeping me grounded.

As for the wrestling, I'll start with some of the legends whom I watched with awe sitting in the front row at the Victoria Pavilion. Archie the Stomper Gouldie, Dory Funk Jr., Harley Race, Sweet Daddy Siki, Abdulah the Butcher and Dan Kroffat. I've always felt that I've learned the art of wrestling from them. But as I eventually felt the tug that pulled me into my own orbit in pro wrestling, I want to thank Mr. Hito and Mr. Sakurada, the two Japanese wrestlers who gave up so much of their valuable time to teach me the art of professional wrestling. I was really taught well. How to fall, how to protect myself, and to have respect for my craft, my opponents, and myself. To an old wrestler named Norman Fredrick Charles III who calmed a nervous kid down when I climbed into the ring for my first matches. Leo Burke gave me the chance to work with him and learn from him. He was one of the best who taught me to love a great match. The Dynamite Kid, Tom Billington, who literally changed wrestling, who pound for pound was the greatest wrestler that ever lived. His absence, as my career took off, just wasn't fair. He was awesome.

When I got to the WWF I was allowed to hang out with the best workers of that era and I'm forever grateful for Cowboy Bob Orton, Don Muraco, the late Adrian Adonis and throughout my career then and now, Roddy Piper. Thank you for your guidance and inspiration.

My tag team partner, Jim (the Anvil) Neidhart, whom I never had an argument with and who made me laugh every single day. He was a true friend through the darkest times. Hulk Hogan, Ric Flair, Ricky Steamboat, Curt Hennig, Randy Savage, The Undertaker, Steve Austin, Mick Foley, Kevin Nash, Sting, Chris Benoit and even Shawn Michaels - the moments I had in the ring with them were my most memorable. To all the guys I ever worked with, I'm grateful. The British Bulldog (Davey Boy Smith), for the match I had in Wembley Stadium - the single best match I ever had. My late brother Owen, for simply being himself. I miss him more every day, but his memory never fades. He was a great kid and a terrific wrestler with a heart of gold and a sense of humor that still makes me smile.

Then there's all the people that most people don't see - Marcy Engelstein, Carlo DeMarco, my management: Bruce Allen, Teri Tkachuk, Gord Kirke and John Gibson, and from Balmur Entertainment, Arnold Gosewich and co-author Perry Lefko.

I especially want to thank my mom and dad whom I love very much. They've got to be the two best parents of all time. To my four children, Jade, Dallas, Alexandra and Blade — thanks for sharing me with all the fans around the world. I want to thank my loving wife Julie for putting up with this whole wacky business. I'd never have made it without her love, encouragement and tremendous sacrifice.

And finally, I want to thank all of my fans for simply being there. Often a fan will tell me how they will never forget me. Well, it's also the other way around. I will never forget you.

I thank you all.

THE TABLE OF
CONTENTS

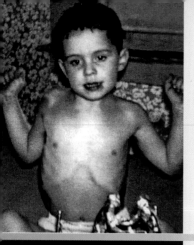

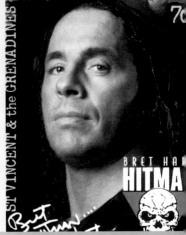

'Rowdy Roddy' Piper is one of Bret Hart's closest and dearest friends. He has known Bret for more than 15 years and was instrumental in helping Bret hone his skills in professional wrestling. Roddy, as a professional wrestler, has won more than 21 championships during his career, including the Light Heavyweight Championship of the World at the age of 19. He is also renowned for his bagpiping skill and was fifth in the World Championship of Bagpiping at age 15. His career has also extended into acting. Roddy currently lives in Portland, Oregon.

PREFACE

BY RODDY PIPER

The smoke-filled, 14,000-seat arena was at a hush. I said to myself as I warmed up for my main-event match, "Isn't there a match going on?" I peeked out from behind the curtain backstage at **Maple Leaf Gardens** and saw an old time wrestler in the ring with a newcomer to **WWF**. His skin was bleach white, and on his well-conditioned body he had on the oldest pair of tights (pale blue to match the skin color) I've seen in years. The tights looked as though he had borrowed them from his father. ■

The oldtime wrestler competing with him was trying every dirty trick in the book to make him look as stupid as the jealous oldtimer could. As I watched I started to feel for this newcomer and watched him struggle to a 20-minute draw.

The kid came back to the dressing room, head hung low, embarrassed by his performance. He sat, staring at the floor. I came up to him and said, "What's your name?"

He slowly looked up and quietly said, "Bret Hart."

I said, "Is Stu your dad?"

"Yes," he said, "yes."

Then I realized why he took the match so hard. He had the weight of a real-life, legendary wrestling family on his shoulders. Everyone expected perfection from Bret. After all, he was a Hart!

I said to him, "Next time you wrestle that oldtimer go for his right knee, it's been bad for years." I told him, "You should be proud of yourself, not down. That old jerk does that to all the new boys. You didn't retreat or surrender and I thought you did great."

A week later I was warming up for my main event in New York and I saw Bret head for the ring. I followed him to the curtain and sure enough he was wrestling the same old jerk. This time Bret dived for the right knee and beat him in a minute and a half. I smiled to myself and thought that's the sign of a champion; he listens, learns and produces. As I was putting on my gear 10 minutes before my match, there was a knock on my dressing-room door. It was Bret. Quiet and respectful as always he said, "I just wanted to say thanks."

I looked in his eyes — I have a knack for being able to read people — and saw a very giving, honest, straight-up man full of pride. I liked him immediately. I said, "How are you getting back to your hotel?"

He said, "I'm calling a taxi."

I said, "After my match, go to my limo and I'll drop you off." A lifelong friendship began.

Bret would ask me questions all the time about this promoter, that hold. I would do my best to to explain it all to him. He was worth the time! Very few are.

One day he came up to me with a gleam in his eye and explained to me a story his dad had told him with facts about me impossible to know. You see, no one knows my childhood or past, and for Stu to tell Bret these facts blew me away. I was a second cousin to Stu and the Hart family. I was stunned. I didn't have any family I knew of at all. I had been on my own since I was 13 years old. Bret said, "You have to come meet my family." This was something I never would do, go to meet people. I am socially retarded and have far too many hang-ups. The more I tried to explain this, the more insistent he was, I went.

First I met Mrs. Hart whom I fell in love with immediately. She had grace, and soft, gentle understanding; then Stu, for whom I had a great deal of respect, and to get that from me you have to be a man's man, then Owen, who made me laugh and feel as if I was one of the 13 kids. What a marvelous family! Two days later I sent Mrs. Hart 12 red roses. I love that lady.

As time went on I watched Bret start to grow in leaps and bounds. We became very close, riding together, me advising him.

One time in Frisco, Bret and his lovely wife, Julie, had checked into the same hotel as me. Bret left his wife in the room just to run down to the front desk. I saw him and said, "Just one drink." Three hours later we were staggering back to our rooms, which hap-pened to be six doors down from each other. I said, "I have two more beers in my room."

He said in a slur, "I've got to get back."

11

I opened my door, and waistlocked him into the room. That started a one-and-three-quarter hour amateur wrestling match. Finally, security sheepishly came to my door with a tray full of beer that was ours if we would stop. We stopped, drank the beer and started again.

About 4:30 a.m. Bret, finally battle worn, headed for his room where the real fight started. Bret's wife had been waiting almost five hours for Bret to get a pen from the front desk.

Bret and I shared many a time, some glorious, some tragic, and always we were there for each other.

Then it happened. Market Square Arena, Indianapolis — Wreslemania VIII. They wanted me to fight Bret. I was stunned, and on national TV told Bret to his face I didn't want to fight him. I didn't want to hurt him. I was the Intercontinental Champion at the time, but the promoters and fans wanted it. Like that, this great friendship had stopped. Finished. You see I play for keeps. I'm known for my wild, fearless, no-mercy style of wrestling. I came to the ring in Indianapolis and to my surprise the crowd was cheering more for Bret than me. As I walked to the ring I could only think of that bleach-white, skinny guy I first saw.

The bell rang and I came out of the hole and started beating Bret until I had him on the mat bleeding. I held nothing back. The fans were screaming Bret's name, girls were crying, fans cursing me. Bret kept getting up. He wouldn't quit.

The fans were now in a frenzy. Bret came at me with a quick dive to my right leg. Ironic, I taught him that one. A flurry of lefts, rights, slams fell on me. I was hurting, tiring, but came back at Bret only to accidentally knock the referee down with Bret's body. I looked and saw the ICC belt on the timekeeper's table. I grabbed it and raised it above my head to finish Bret. But the fans were screaming in a pleading way, "Don't hit him, please don't!"

I paused, looked and threw the belt back. I grabbed Bret and put the Sleeper hold on him. He was gone. I yelled for the ref to check him. As the ref got up, Bret kicked the turnbuckle pushing me back on the mat. I still had the Sleeper on Bret, but my shoulders were on the mat. The referee crawled over, the fans sat stunned. I thought the ref would check Bret, but instead he counted "1, 2, 3," as I realized my shoulders were on the mat. It was the first time my shoulders were ever pinned in the WWF.

I stood up and watched in disbelief the ref raising Bret's hand while fans screamed with joy.

I paused, and picked up the ICC belt. Bret stood wobbly. I said, "Turn around, kid." I buckled the belt on him. He didn't need my help anymore.

Bret went on to earn belt after belt, the fans behind him all the way. Why? Because he earned it honestly and the hard way and he made a fan out of me

Ever forward, Bret!

Rowdy Roddy Piper

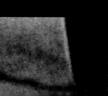

Another one bites the dust.
Hitman is U. S. champion.

14

THE LEGEND OF
BRET HART

In the ever-changing world of professional wrestling, one international performer has stood the test of time.

Bret "Hitman" Hart.

The Canadian icon from Calgary, Alberta has grappled with the greatest on the globe, proving himself as The Excellence Of Execution in the squared circle.

His technical and athletic ability, punctuated by his patented Sharpshooter submission move, have earned him the right to proclaim himself The Best There Is, The Best There Was, The Best There Ever Will Be.

Superstar Rocky Maivia — The Rock — paid Bret the ultimate compliment when he referred to him as a "legend" in an nationally-televised interview in 1999. ■

And, it's no surprise why. Few wrestlers have made an impact in the sport inside and outside of the ring such as The Hitman. Fifteen championship belts collected in the World Wrestling Federation and World Championship Wrestling are the hardware on which he can hang his fame.

His career includes assorted other achievements. He ranked No. 1 in 1993 and 1994 in *Pro Wrestling Illustrated's* top 500 listings. The mat magazine acclaimed him the Best Bad Guy wrestler in 1997, when he also received the award for Comeback of the Year and Match of the Year (with Stone Cold Steve Austin). In 1994, he won the Most Inspirational Award.

Yet his place in wrestling history goes far beyond his accomplishments in the ring. During a critical switch in the 1990s, the WWF turned to Bret to showcase stars of skill and athleticism compared to the big, brawny performers of the previous decade.

Kathy Dowd wrote in the inaugural issue of *Toxxxic* magazine that Bret and his late brother Owen redefined technical wrestling in the 1990s, "literally saving the WWF from a glut of musclebound goons dominating the landscape."

Standing 6-feet, 230 pounds, Bret has lacked the height and weight of many of his premier opponents, but has compensated with skill and savvy. The Wrestling Analyst wrote this about Bret in its January, 1999 issue: "The Hitman must know every maneuver, hold and counter ever invented." Moreover, the magazine gave him a perfect 10 on his ring science: "Hart's true talent is his knack for using mat science to conceal physical problems. If his knees are aching, he will keep the action down on the mat with hammerlocks or armbars. If an elbow is hindering him, he'll use leglocks. It's difficult to maintain an advantage over him on the mat for long."

"Hart's true talent is his knack for using mat science to conceal physical problems . . . It's difficult to maintain an advantage over him on the mat for long."

Bret in his role as **Luther Root** in the Lonesome Dove series on the set in November of 1994.

Some of the greatest matches in the '90s involve Bret: SummerSlam '92, featuring the battle with his brother-in-law The British Bulldog (Davey Boy Smith); Wrestlemania 12, the Ironman Match with Shawn Michaels; Wrestlemania 13 against a bloodied Stone Cold Steve Austin; SummerSlam '97 against The Undertaker. Not only did Bret show his ability, he helped bring out the best in his opponents.

Bret understands professionalism, having missed only two WWF cards in 14 years, including painful personal periods such as the deaths of his brother Dean in 1991 and good friend Brian Pillman in 1997.

Bret also battled through a chronic bad right knee that took a beating in a classic match against Stone Cold Steve Austin in 1997.

Promoters knew they could count on Bret to show up and give fans their money's worth. Some promoters refused to book cards unless assured of Bret's availability.

He became the key figure in the battle between the World Wrestling Federation and World Championship Wrestling, both of which wanted him and made him the subject of the biggest bidding war in the history of the business.

His dramatic split from the WWF to the WCW rated as the top news story of 1997 by *Pro Wrestling Illustrated* in its 1998 Wrestling Almanac.

"When the history of the war between the WWF and WCW is examined, this will surely be listed as one of the turning points," *PWI* wrote.

"The wrestlers will always see to it that I'm respected for what I put in."

CHALLENGE
...7-7176 or (780) 975-5311

Bret "loses" his "match" to country singer Paul Brandt at the Calgary Stampede in July of 1999.

Bret's career has given him fame and fortune that he could never have imagined. In 1991, the *Alberta Report* acclaimed him the most famous Albertan in the world. His popularity has allowed him to be a guest three times at the White House and he has personal autographs from U.S. Presidents Bill Clinton and George Bush. Bret has met such celebrities as Bruce Springsteen, Neil Young, Pamela Anderson, Burt Reynolds, Donald Trump and Wayne Gretzky, to name but a few. Aaron Neville, lead singer of the New Orleans-based Neville Brothers, is among his better friends. Bret inspired and performed in a music video by the hip hop group The Rascalz.

The Yankee Clipper, Joe DiMaggio, who closely guarded his privacy, insisted on having his picture taken with Bret.

Bret's popularity has carried over to other television and film credits. The Hitman has portrayed his character on *The Simpsons* and *MAD TV*. In fact, he has incorporated *MAD TV's* Will Sasso into some of his wrestling shows with the WCW.

He also appeared on several episodes of the *Lonesome Dove* television series in 1994 and '95 and had been slated to be a regular on the highly acclaimed show in '96, except it was canceled due to rising costs.

. . . the *Alberta Report* acclaimed him the most famous Albertan in the world

Bret with some of his great celebrity friends — Pamela Anderson Lee, Wayne Gretzky, Kirk Muller, and Howard Stern.

NO CHOC
202 132.28
LONESOME DOVE
TRAVELLER A8A6
M. KEUSCH
R. STANNETT 11 01 94
34A 2

Bret studies his lines on the set of
Lonesome Dove for his upcoming
scenes.

The documentary about Bret's life called *Wrestling With Shadows*, by High Road Productions, received critical acclaim upon its release in 1998 and subsequently won several awards. The film dealt with family values meshed into the culture, business and politics of wrestling. Bret's portrayal in the film accomplished for wrestling what Arnold Schwarzenegger did for bodybuilding in the documentary *Pumping Iron*. Bret told the truth in a sport which has been criticized for being fake.

"People talk about wrestling not being real," he said in the documentary's opening minutes. "It's far more real than people think."

Movie critics who don't know an armlock from a headlock lauded Bret for his insights. What Bret tried to convey is that even though the results are almost always pre-determined, there's a certain artistry to making the show believable. Bret has always tried to put as much thought into the artistic side of the match as the physical side. The wrestling ring is the canvas upon which he creates his images.

"People talk about wrestling not being real, ... It's far more real than people think."

Bret has paved the way for stars such as The Rock and many of his generation by standing up for the rights of wrestlers. More than that, Bret taught the likes of many current stars such as Edge, Test, Ken Shamrock and Mark Henry.

"The wrestlers will always see to it that I'm respected for what I put in," Bret says. "Very few guys worked as hard as I did in the ring and I think the wrestlers know that and I think that's the most important thing in the world for me."

He has also given unselfishly of his time and energy to various international charities. He is involved with Special Olympics, the Cancer Society, the Kidney Foundation and Make A Wish Foundation. He has also supported Calgary charities such as the Children's Hospital Foundation, For The Love Of Children and Street Teens.

Bret has tried to remain true to himself and his Hitman character, fighting inside and outside of the ring for what he believes to be right.

He has been criticized by some industry officials, observers and fellow wrestlers for taking the business too seriously, but there's also a strong faction who respect him for his beliefs.

Bret autographs a fan's specially made Canadian Championship belt.

What has endeared **Bret** to people who passionately follow wrestling and even those who only have a limited understanding of it, is his honesty, which he gained from a solid grounding growing up in the first family of wrestling.

One of the rare photographs of all the Hart boys together with their dad, Stu.

Bret's first "publicity" photo about the age of four in his dad's house.

BORN TO BE A
WRESTLER

Born July 2, 1957, Bret grew up surrounded by seven brothers and four sisters in a 21-room domain with a sign outside that reads Hart House. The home often had wrestlers training in the basement which became known as the Dungeon. Collectively, it certainly prepared Bret for a different kind of life.

Some might even call it bizarre.

Bret's parents, Stu and Helen, purchased the house — which once served as an army hospital in World War I — in 1948. Stu owned and operated Stampede Wrestling, a circuit which had its base in Calgary but also extended throughout western Canada and occasionally forayed into distant places such as Alaska. Helen never liked the business but dutifully supported her husband by doing bookkeeping, promotional work and cooking for the family and the wrestlers. ■

About a year after buying the house, Stu filled the basement with various weights, rowing machines and assorted other innovative exercise apparatus and covered the floor with mats that had little cushion. The pungent smell of sweat filled the room, which had the sounds of grapplers grunting and groaning while they stretched their muscles and limbs. Anyone who aspired to wrestle in Stu's circuit had to prove himself against the Hart patriarch.

The Dungeon became the most respected and infamous wrestling school in North America. It also sparked a spinoff of Hart Brothers Wrestling Schools.

Stu filled the basement with various weights, rowing machines and assorted other innovative exercise apparatus and covered the floor with mats that had little cushion.

Stu cranks it up with **Bret** in his famous headlock.

SMITH

BRUCE

KEITH

HELEN

ROC

WAYNE

Family photo prior to Owen's birth during Calgary Stampede Week in 1964.

RCIANO

STU

DEAN

ELLIE

GEORGIA

BRET

ALISON

ROSS

33

Stu received his wrestling education squaring off against salty types known as Shooters. They specialized in submission moves that could easily produce broken limbs and strained muscles. To survive against these grizzly grapplers, a person needed to be tough.

You might say Bret was born to be a wrestler or, at the very least, an athlete. Stu won a Canadian amateur wrestling championship, then graduated to the professional circuit, while also playing a year in the Canadian Football League with the Edmonton Eskimos. Bret's maternal grandfather, Harry J. Smith, excelled in the marathon and qualified for the American team in the 1912 Olympics, but missed the competition due to an ankle injury.

Bret received his first exposure to his father's shows at the tender age of 4 1/2. He sold programs and when that was done he'd take a seat in between the two timekeepers. He easily had the best view in the building.

"It was a very privileged position right from the beginning," Bret says.

"Every Hart brother was down there, but it would be the brother ahead of you whose strict job it was to watch you. It was pretty effortless, you'd just go down and basically just watch the wrestling. When I was really small, I'd get pretty tired by about 11 o'clock."

"Every Hart brother was down there, but it would be the brother ahead of you whose strict job it was to watch you."

Merry Christmas

The Stewart & Hart Family

Similar to his brothers, Bret learned not only to defend himself, but to defend wrestling from kids who called the sport and his father a fake. Often Bret had to wrestle to prove his point.

"As a kid I thought I couldn't lose," Bret says. "It was impossible, you were supposed to win. I had it ingrained in me that my dad was a wrestler and it was passed down. Maybe it was."

Bret had a quiet, unassuming presence in school, but developed a profound reputation at his dad's shows. During the intermissions, the Hart brothers often challenged other kids to matches, which drew crowds of young admirers. The Harts often won their bouts and commanded respect with the girls.

Bret won the city championship the following year, but lost the provincial when he broke a collarbone in a match and required a sling for about four months. Bret recovered to win the city and provincial the next two years.

"As a kid I thought I couldn't lose," Bret says.

"It was impossible, you were supposed to win."

"I had a completely altered image than I had at school," Bret says. "No girls took interest in me at all, whereas at wrestling matches I'd go around the corner and a mob of them would run up to me. I kind of had the run of the place even at a very young age. It didn't mean anything, but at the same time I had a whole different persona, which I think affected me a lot."

Bret began amateur wrestling at the YMCA at about the age of nine. He didn't start competing until junior high school and really only did it to impress Stu, knowing it meant a lot to him. Bret won the city championship in Grade 11, but lost the provincial when he broke a collarbone in a match and wore a sling for several months. Bret recovered to win the city and provincial the next two years.

While the wrestling community pushed him to continue and try to crack Canada's team for the Commonwealth Games, Bret had other ideas.

While early in his youth Bret drew a cartoon of himself as the champion of the world in a fictitious circuit called the Worldwide Wrestling Federation. He wanted a future as a film director. He took a year and a half off after graduation from Ernest Manning High School and labored at a gas plant to pay for his tuition at Mount Royal College.

Bret gave college wrestling a try and won his weight championship. While the wrestling community pushed him to continue and try to crack Canada's team for the Commonwealth Games, Bret had other ideas. He hated having to make weight all the time and didn't see a future in the sport.

"It was more like joining a monastery," he says. "It was just not my idea of a good time. I loved what I did in amateur wrestling and I'm proud of what I accomplished in the limited time I was in it, but I thought if you pursued it you'd just end up being an old amateur wrestling coach or phys-ed teacher at a high school and I didn't want to be like that."

One of Bret's early matches with Stampede against Mike Sharpe in 1979.

Bret bombed in college, feeling lost from the start when his friend, Jim Cummings, who had enrolled in the same program, quit the day before the semester started. Compounded with the time he devoted to wrestling, Bret knew he'd basically have to start the program all over again the following year, but lacked money.

"I was really properly schooled and educated in pro wrestling," Bret says. "I don't know if anybody was taught as well as I was."

His principal occupation was refereeing in the evenings for Stu in small towns close to home.

During that period Bret learned to wrestle professionally from two Japanese men, Mr. Hito and Mr. Sakurada, who worked for Stu. Bret figured he could learn the basics in three or four days and travel to some circuits and earn some money. He quickly discovered it took serious work and dedication. Bret's tutors put him through gruelling sessions for about five hours a day, teaching him headlocks, body slams and hip tosses. The workouts concluded with Bret's teachers throwing him 50 different ways. After only a few weeks of training he developed great timing and ability and became a fine-tuned machine.

"I was really properly schooled and educated in pro wrestling," Bret says. "I don't know if anybody was taught as well as I was."

A GOOD GUY FROM CALGARY

TURNING PRO

Bret's pro career began in 1978, working a handful of cards for Stu in Western Canada, and took an exotic turn when he joined his eldest brother Smith wrestling in Puerto Rico for three months.

Upon his return, Bret worked full-time for Stu. Bret and his brother-in-law Tommy Billington — The Dynamite Kid — engaged in some classic matches. Bret worked as the babyface, while The Dynamite Kid acted as the heel. Bret credits The Dynamite Kid with having a profound impact on the junior heavyweight division, which had a higher profile at the time than the heavyweights. ■

Bret won the British Commonwealth Championship as a solo performer and the tag-team title numerous times with his brother, Keith. After working more than two years in North America, Bret started working internationally in countries such as Japan, Germany and England, alternating between being a heel and hero, depending on the country. In Germany he portrayed a good guy, but in England he reversed his role and became the bad cowboy from Calgary.

Bret preferred the role of a heel, which he found more fun than being a babyface, but his youthful looks made him more suited to portraying a good guy. Bret eventually won the first of several North American titles when he became a recognized heavyweight at about the 220-pound level.

"I was just a good guy from Calgary and you could hear a pin drop when they announced me"

May, 1999 – Hitman hoists President's Cup in Calgary at the Saddledome when Hitmen Hockey Team won WHL Championship.

"My dad wrestled this female tiger during Stampede week about 1970 much to the surprise and chagrin of my mom."

He became Stu's top draw from that point forward and one of his leading good guys, who didn't carry the same appeal as the villains. As Bret's weight increased to 230 and his skills improved, he figured he could work anywhere.

In July, 1984, George Scott approached Stu on behalf of Vince McMahon Jr. to take over Stampede Wrestling. McMahon had purchased Capitol Wrestling Corporation from his father and his partners in June, 1982 and started expanding his power by taking out independant promoters such as Stu to strengthen the World Wrestling Federation.

It had all the makings of a great deal because it guaranteed Stu income without the financial risk of being his own operator.

During that period, wrestling was broken up into territories across North America. If a regional promoter didn't sell his operation or make a deal with McMahon, he literally forced them out of the game. Some people went quietly, others did not. McMahon also went in and signed many wrestlers away from these promotions, luring them with promises of national television exposure. It changed the course of wrestling history and its business.

Part of the deal with Stu included Bret and his brothers-in-law The Dynamite Kid, Jim (The Anvil) Neidhart and Davey Boy Smith joining the WWF. The plan also called for one of Bret's other seven brothers, Bruce, who now operates Stampede Wrestling, to work in a management capacity for the WWF. It had all the makings of a great deal because it guaranteed Stu income without the financial risk of being his own operator.

Bret with a bloodied face being helped by Robbie Stewart, Davey Boy Smith and Randy Tyler during Stampede Wrestling.

Dr. David Schultz on the receiving end of Bret's "hold" during Stampede Wrestling in 1982.

Bret had to take a back seat to the WWF's array of babyfaces.

Bret had cartilage surgery on his right knee shortly afterward and couldn't do much, but did a tour of Japan for five weeks beginning in the middle of August. The day he returned he began a four-day stretch in Calgary, Edmonton, Vancouver and Winnipeg. Bret didn't have much of a profile early in his WWF career, usually opening the shows when the fans barely settled in their seats.

"I was just a good guy from Calgary and you could hear a pin drop when they announced me," he says. "Nobody knew who I was or cared. I just couldn't get anywhere past that. I just sort of wilted in the background. I couldn't get any exposure at all."

Bret had to take a back seat to the WWF's array of babyfaces such as Ricky (The Dragon) Steamboat, Jake (The Snake) Roberts, The Junkyard Dog and Hulk Hogan, who became the promotion's top attraction.

One night in February, 1985, the WWF braintrust approached Bret with the idea of creating a new version of Cowboy Bret Hart — complete with chaps, spurs, a cowboy hat that lit up and cowboy music. He would be the WWF's version of The Electric Horseman with his own horse at every show.

The plan called for the marketing of toys, dolls and action figures, from which Bret would collect a percentage of the sales.

The idea seemed exciting at first to Bret, who yearned for a bigger presence, but he just couldn't buy into the character. Bret didn't like country music, hated cowboy boots because they hurt his knees and hadn't ridden a horse much in his life. At about one in the morning he approached George Scott and begged out of the cowboy idea saying it would be an insult to real cowboys such as the ones who lived in his home town. Scott initially scoffed but gave way.

Bret didn't have much of a profile early in his WWF career, usually opening the shows when the fans barely settled in their seats.

Bret then put forth an idea that would launch his WWF profile. He suggested hooking up with Jim Neidhart, who wrestled in singles competition with Jimmy (The Mouth of the South) Hart as his manager, and turning into a bad guy. Collectively they could be known as the Hart Foundation. Scott laughed off the idea because he didn't think Bret had the face or the attitude to be a heel.

For the next month Bret continued to plummet in the WWF and sensed he had limited time in it.

One of Bret's hardest fought matches in his early days was against Archie "The Stomper" Gouldie about 1983.

Bret gives Duke Myers a "no-brainer" with a chair in a match in Regina in 1981.

Hitman puts the squeeze on Dallas Page in Vegas, 1998

EXCELLENCE OF
EXECUTION

Early in March, 1985, about three weeks before the inaugural Wrestlemania, the event that sprung the WWF to mainstream commercial status, Bret called to quit. He figured the WWF management expected it anyway, but much to his surprise it decided to go ahead with his idea to join with Jim Neidhart as bad guys.

Bret hadn't even talked to Neidhart about it, so he felt sheepish going to him and asking for his approval. Neidhart thought it could work, but Bret felt as though he was riding on his brother-in-law's coattails.

"I knew I could wrestle but I just didn't have any support from anybody. No one else thought I could," Bret says. "I didn't need anybody to make me. I could make myself. I turned my career around. It was the best thing I ever did." ■

Bret adopted the name "Hitman." Because of the diversity of Bret's wrestling arsenal, announcer Gorilla Monsoon dubbed him The Excellence Of Execution. It identified Bret as much as Hitman and helped develop his character and charisma.

The added ingredient was the color pink. The duo started out with black and blue uniforms, but switched to pink to draw heat from the audience as heels. They began with a stripe of pink up the sides of their tights and unveiled their new-look uniforms at a card in San Diego in the fall of 1986. McMahon couldn't believe it when he saw them backstage.

"He walked around us and said 'don't ever change this color, this is you, this is your color from now on. This is the one thing you guys have been missing since you've been here. You've had no color. Now you have color'."

Bret and good friend Aaron Neville

The added ingredient
was the color pink

Jimmy Hart loved it. In the WWF video about the Hart Foundation, the silver-tongued former singer of the '70s rock group The Gentrys said: "These guys are the only guys bad enough to walk down the streets of any city in the world and wear pink and get by with it."

On Jan. 26, 1987, the Hart Foundation won its first championship beating The British Bulldogs — Davey Boy Smith and Tommy Billington — in Tampa, Florida with some dastardly help from The Mouth Of The South and referee Danny Davis, a future member of the Hart Foundation. While Davis tended to The Dynamite Kid outside the ring after Jimmy Hart knocked him silly with his megaphone, the Hart Foundation worked on Davey Boy. The end came when the Anvil had Davey Boy in a bear hug and Bret dropped him with a running clothesline — the Hart Foundation's finishing move known as The Hart Attack — to set up the pin.

"These guys are the only guys bad enough to walk down the streets of any city in the world and wear pink and get by with it."

Bret adopted the name "Hitman".

Hitman blasts Booker "T".

Hitman finishes off Lex Luger.

The championships raised the Hart Foundation's profile, which meant added time to do arena and pay-per-view TV interviews. Bret says these compromise 50% of what it takes to make it as a wrestler. Bret felt nervous and intimidated watching the likes of Hogan, Junkyard Dog and King Kong Bundy take to the TV with ease. The first time he and Neidhart did an interview, someone made a noise in the background, which required repeating the segment. While he watched a replay of it, Bret noticed his eyes flashing and darting all over the place because of his nervousness.

Bret quickly excused himself and ran to the dressing room and retrieved some mirrored sunglasses he wore from that point forward in interviews. He assumed a laidback and cool persona behind his sunglasses, saying little in interviews. It took Bret at least a year to overcome his shyness and develop character and personality.

Hitman gets ready to counter the scorpion/sharpshooter in a classic confrontation with Sting in Toronto.

The end is near as Hitman applies his Sharpshooter once again.

"I didn't need anybody to make me. I could make myself. I turned my career around. It was the best thing I ever did."

Bret started a habit of walking down the aisle and slowly handing his shades to youngsters. As the fans became more comfortable with what he was doing, Bret leaned over and placed the glasses on them. It became more profound when he started doing it with wraparound sunglasses. He and Neidhart proclaimed themselves as the best tag team ever, which spawned an expression — The Best There Is, The Best There Was, The Best There Ever Will Be — that became part of Bret's routine. He used it in his television monologues, sometimes in the middle of it or often at the end for more effect.

The Hart Foundation lost its tag-team title nine months later to Strike Force — Rick Martel and Tito Santana — in Syracuse, but reclaimed the belts beating Demolition at SummerSlam '90. By this time, they had changed from heels to heroes, leading to pivotal match nine months later in Los Angeles at Wrestlemania 7 against the Nasty Boys, managed dutifully by Jimmy Hart. The former manager of the Hart Foundation played the spoiler role to perfection by helping dethrone the team he helped build with underhanded tactics.

Hitman and his loyal Canadian fans.

Hitman plows through Lex Luger and Rick Steiner with a double-clothesline.

GOING SOLO

The loss to the **Nasty Boys** ended **Bret's** tag team affiliation with **Neidhart** and dissolved the **Hart Foundation** (although **Bret** and **Owen** teamed up later on as the New Foundation). It also spawned **Bret's** career as principally a solo performer and springboarded his rise to the top.

In August, 1991, some five months after the tag team loss at Wrestlemania, **Bret** received a shot at the Intercontinental championship belt held by **Curt (Mr. Perfect) Hennig.** With **Stu** and **Helen Hart** in attendance, the match took place at **SummerSlam** in New York's **Madison Square Garden,** a venue in which **Bret** would have some of the best bouts of his career. ■

Bret had developed quite a fashion flair by this point and entered the ring wearing a pink leather jacket with black epaulets. He and Hennig battled through a bout that went back and forth. Hennig used his Perfect-plex to try and win but Bret wriggled out. As the fans started a deafening chant of "Let's Go, Bret," the challenger beat the champion with the Sharpshooter. It turned out to be an early-classic match of Bret's career against an opponent who developed into one of the best of all time.

In January, 1992 Bret lost the I.C. title to The Mountie — Jacques Rougeau — in Springfield, Massachusetts. Two days later, Rougeau lost to Rowdy Roddy Piper, who surrendered the title almost three months later to Bret in a battle of two good guys at Wrestlemania 8. In the interview beforehand, Piper joked he knew Bret since he was "knee-high to a grasshopper." Bret pushed Piper, signifying he didn't appreciate the comments from the king of the kilt. The two legends produced a classic match in which Piper bloodied Bret. Piper appeared to have him beat with his Sleeper finishing move, but Bret bounced out of it by pushing off the turnbuckle with his legs and flipping over the champion for the three count. Piper gave Bret a lift off the canvas and placed the belt around him.

A stunning photo of Sting on the receiving end of the Sharpshooter.

Bret realized he had more ability than any wrestler in the company and deserved to be champion again.

Hitman works the leg.

Two days later, Rougeau lost to Rowdy Roddy Piper, who surrendered the title almost three months later to Bret in a battle of two good guys at Wrestlemania 8. In the interview before-hand, Piper joked he knew Bret since he was "knee-high to a grasshopper." Bret pushed Piper, signifying he didn't appreciate the comments from the king of the kilt.

Hitman in action dropping
an elbow on D.D.P.'s knee.

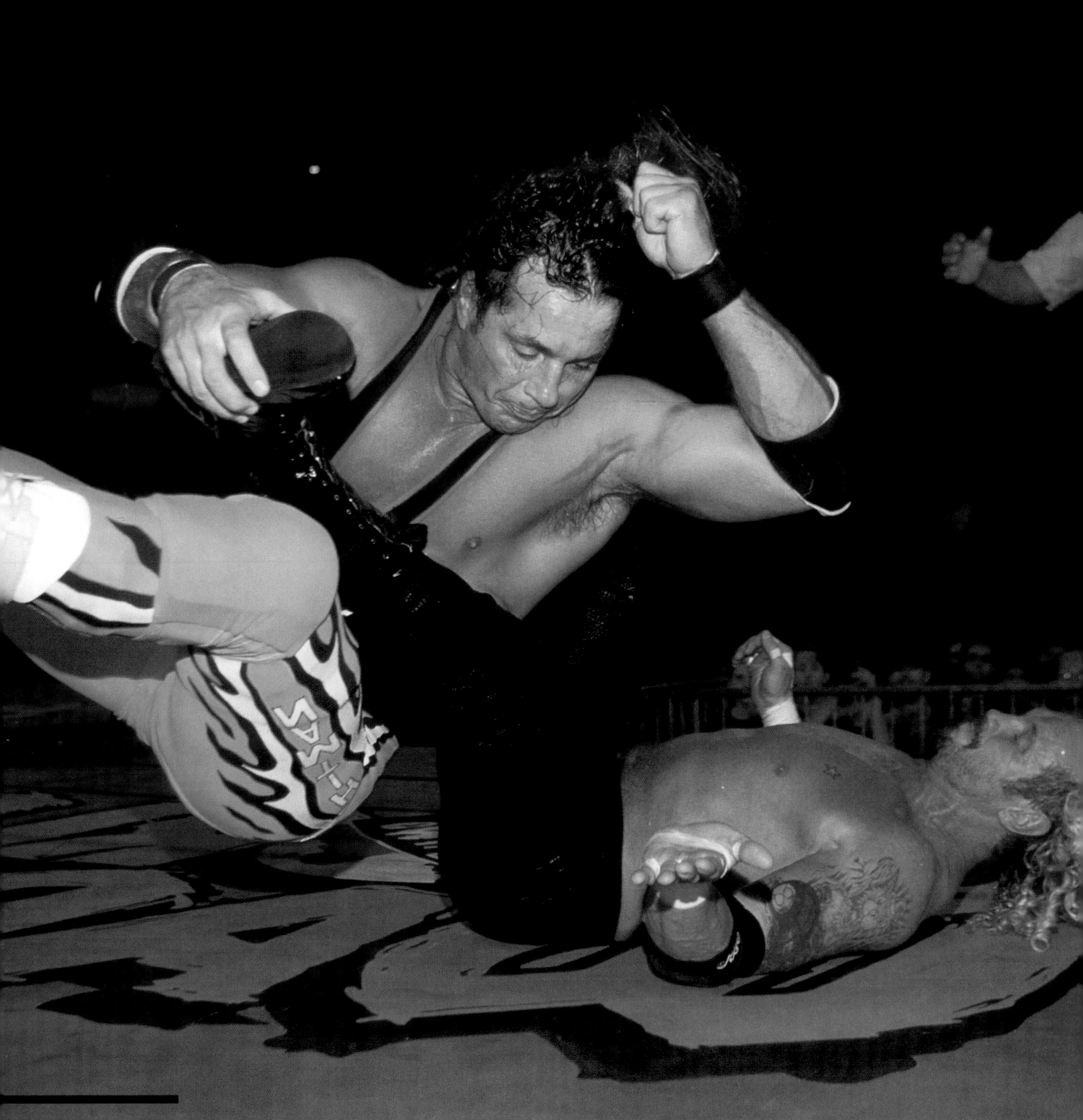

That led to a showdown at SummerSlam in August, 1992 between Bret and Davey Boy Smith at Wembley Stadium in the British Bulldog's native country. This was the first time the annual WWF event was held outside of the United States.

It evolved into one of the greatest matches in the careers of both wrestlers, witnessed by 80,355, the second-biggest crowd in WWF history. The storyline pitted two brothers-in-law, whose feud had torn the family apart. Piper started off the pomp and circumstance by joining the Balmoral Highlander bagpipers in a rendition of Scotland The Brave.

In cutting a promo backstage, Davey Boy said: "When I step into the ring with you, Bret, I never met you. I don't even know you." Bret fired back in his segment by saying: "The British Bulldog has the gall to say he's never met me. He doesn't know me. Take a good look at my face and say you don't know me. Look me in the eye. I introduced you to my sister (Diana) in the first place. I'm the one that helped you. You wouldn't be where you are if it wasn't for me."

The storyline pitted two brothers-in-law, whose feud had torn the family apart. Piper started off the pomp and circumstance by joining the Balmoral Highlander bagpipers in a rendition of Scotland The Brave.

Bret said The British Bulldog started the tension that frayed away at the family and boldly predicted the following day his brother-in-law was going to think he woke up in the dungeon at Windsor Castle. Interviewed before her brother and brother-in-law entered the ring, Diana said she loved them both and had no concern who won, that the family bond was greater than anything. "It's more valuable to me than anything. Nothing can even replace that, not even the Intercontinental belt."

Both wrestlers combined in a clinic demonstrating just about every power and finesse move imaginable. Bret tried to win it with a Sunset Flip, but Davey Boy reversed it for the three count.

The show didn't end there. Davey Boy extended his hand in friendship to Bret, who turned his back on his brother-in-law, eliciting boos from the crowd. Bret then turned around and accepted the handshake and gave Davey Boy a hug. Diana joined in and fireworks ended the spectacle.

Bret believes that match made him. With his fan popularity soaring and the WWF moving away from the muscle-builders and hulks, Bret was headed for the Heavyweight championship. It was clear to those in the industry he was clearly the top wrestler in the game, recognized for his realism and dramatic matches.

"I was chosen as the guy that was very clean and wholesome and you could take my character and sort of put it up to the light and I wouldn't cause any problems for the company," he says.

After winning and losing the Intercontinental title twice, Bret's crowning moment came in Saskatoon, Saskatchewan on Oct. 12, 1992 in a non-televised house match against Ric (The Nature Boy) Flair, who beat Randy (Macho Man) Savage for the Heavyweight title the previous month. Bret used the Sharpshooter to force The Nature Boy to give up.

"All of a sudden it was like I woke up one day and was heavyweight champion of the world," Bret says. "I kept thinking that somebody else should be the champion,."

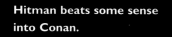
Hitman beats some sense into Conan.

He became a fighting champion, taking on all comers, including The Heartbreak Kid (Shawn Michaels), the Intercontinental titleholder at the time.

In April, 1994, Bret lost the title to Yokozuna at Wrestlemania 9 in Las Vegas. Yokozuna, who weighed in at 505 pounds and beat his opponents simply by sitting on them, won with the aid of his sinister manager, Mr. Fuji, who threw salt in Bret's eyes. After the match, Hulk Hogan rushed into the ring and won the belt when he beat Yokozuna.

When he lost the title, Bret realized he had more ability than any wrestler in the company and deserved to be champion again. Three months later, Yokozuna beat Hogan to take the title. That spawned a rematch between Bret and the jumbo Japanese wrestler at Wrestlemania 10 in New York in March, 1994. When Bret beat his portly opponent, the good guys emerged from the dressing room and embraced The Hitman in the ring, along with guest announcer Burt Reynolds. Lex Luger and Razor Ramon hoisted Bret on their shoulders.

He became a fighting champion, taking on all comers.

Hitman slaps a rear chin-lock on Sting

A classic! Hitman sharpshoots the Stinger.

"All of a sudden it was like I woke up one day and was heavyweight champion of the world," Bret says.

Hitman runs for cover!

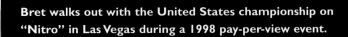

Bret walks out with the United States championship on "Nitro" in Las Vegas during a 1998 pay-per-view event.

WWF TO WCW

THE MOVE

In November, 1994 in San Antonio, Texas, Bret dropped the belt for the second time to the venerable Bob Backlund, who first won the Heavyweight title in 1978. Backlund subsequently dropped the belt to Diesel (Kevin Nash) three days later in New York.

In 1994, Bret realized two childhood dreams: being a cowboy in the wild west and being part of a hockey team. He appeared in a couple episodes of the television show *Lonesome Dove*, which gave him the thrill of the wild west. He also headlined a group, which included hockey stars Theo Fleury and Joe Sakic, that brought major junior hockey back to Calgary with a team known as The Hitmen. The players had Bret's pink, black and white colors as part of their uniforms. ■

he producers of *Lonesome Dove* brought Bret back in 1995 as a semi-regular and, during that period, he won the Heavyweight championship for the third time beating Diesel in the Survivor Series in Landover, Maryland. Bret quickly realized he would only have the belt a short time because McMahon wanted to promote Shawn Michaels.

He also headlined a group that brought major junior hockey back to Calgary with a team known as The Hitmen.

Bret celebrates with members of the Hitmen hockey team after winning the Presidents Cup in Calgary in May, 1999.

Bret had been preparing for a full-time role as the sheriff in his third season on *Lonesome Dove.*

Bret in his role as Luther Root riding shot-gun on the stagecoach during the second season of Lonesome Dove.

Bret had been preparing for a full-time role as the sheriff in his third season on Lonesome Dove, which was slated to begin shooting the following April, shortly after Wrestlemania 12 in Anaheim, California. Bret worked out with a personal-fitness instructor and weight-training coach to prepare himself for one of the most physically-demanding matches of his career.

The March, 1995 issue of WWF Magazine featured Bret on the cover with a photo of him on location of the set of Lonesome Dove and titled the story: It's High Noon For The Hitman.

While Bret didn't care so much about leaving wrestling and possibly not returning, he noticed a change in which the wrong players had seized power, in his opinion. As far as he was concerned, a questionable government was about to take over headed by Shawn Michaels, whom Bret did not consider a team guy.

The IronMan Championship Match consisted of a 60-minute bout in which the winner would be the person who had the most decisions by either a pinfall, submission, countout or disqualification. Shawn Michaels skirted down to the ring from a harness high above the crowd. McMahon hinted at the Michaels era when he described The Heartbreak Kid as "the leader of a new WWF generation." It would

The March, 1995 issue of *WWF Magazine* featured Bret on the cover with a photo of him on location of the set of *Lonesome Dove* and titled the story: It's High Noon For The Hitman.

become D-Generation X, part of the sleazy direction Bret would publicly lambaste near the end of his WWF tenure. Bret entered the ring wearing a black jacket with pink epaulets and gave his glasses to his youngest son, Blade.

The match went the distance, with Bret trying to force Shawn to submit to the Sharpshooter in the final 40 seconds. When the bell rang without any decisions, Bret walked away with the belt, only to have to come back to fight under sudden-death rules to decide a winner. Shawn won the match a minute later with his Super Kick finishing move called Sweet Chin Music.

Bret's acting plans took an unexpected turn when the network carrying Lonesome Dove cancelled the critically-acclaimed series because of mounting production costs. McMahon wanted Bret back, but he planned to pursue other acting possibilities and give his body and his face a break from the grind of wrestling 300 days a year the last 12 years. Bret didn't plan to return until October at the earliest.

Shortly thereafter, Ted Turner's WCW Nitro began an 83-week run of beating WWF's Raw in the weekly Monday night ratings. In June, Kevin Nash and Scott Hall, who portrayed

The Great Hart and the Great Gretzky.

Bret worked out with a personal-fitness instructor and weight-training coach to prepare himself for one of the most physically-demanding matches of his career.

Bret in action with Sting

Razor Ramon, joined WCW, which started outbidding the WWF for talent and offered guaranteed contracts. Prior to that, wrestlers didn't have contracts.

While in California in September, Bret had a zealous agent/manager who set up a meeting for him with WCW president Eric Bischoff. Bischoff made Bret an offer in which he'd triple his earnings to $3 million a year for three years, making him the second-highest paid performer next to Hogan.

"It was pretty hard not to take the money," Bret says. "I didn't feel I had that much of a loyalty to Vince McMahon. I had a loyalty to my fans."

Bret turned down the WCW offer and signed a 20-year WWF deal paying him significantly less. Bret only had to wrestle for the first three years and then he'd have a high-ranking position in management.

"It was pretty hard not to take the money," Bret says. "I didn't feel I had that much of a loyalty to Vince McMahon. I had a loyalty to my fans."

Bret with his WWF World Title

Bret's return featured a feud with the WWF's new emerging star Stone Cold Steve Austin, the Texan with the bald head, black vest and bad attitude. He was known as Stunning Steve Austin in WCW.

Prodded by McMahon, Bret turned from hero to heel in 1997 and began an anti-American stance, which made him a villain in the U.S. but still a hero in Canada. While Americans cursed him, Canadians embraced him, the highlight coming in Calgary at the Canadian Stampede in July. It featured a match involving the revamped Hart Foundation, which included the late Brian Pillman, The British Bulldog, The Anvil, Owen and Bret against Americans, headlined by Austin. Bret walked out to a thunderous ovation and placed his sunglasses on his mother, Helen. Stu was incorporated into the match which the Canadians won and which was followed by three generations of the Harts joining in the ring.

Shortly thereafter, McMahon told Bret the company was in "financial peril" and could no longer afford to pay him what the contract stipulated. McMahon told Bret to explore his options with WCW making it appear as though the WWF owner was doing his star attraction a favor. That related back to when Bret had been loyal to McMahon after passing up the WCW offer to remain with the WWF. The WCW kept its original offer to Bret and, after much thought, he signed with the WCW.

Bret faces off against Stone Cold Steve Austin

Bret wanted to leave with dignity and on his own terms, which contractually he had the right to do because of the clause that gave him creative control in the final 30 days. He and McMahon debated the issue back and forth and appeared to have reached a compromise, allowing Bret to drop the belt in Ottawa the day after the Survivor Series in Montreal.

His wife, Julie, and the couple's four children — Jade, Dallas, Alexandra and Blade — joined him for what he called probably the biggest fight of his whole life. The anxiety of the pivotal match had been mounting for some time, causing Bret physical and emotional stress. He just wanted to finish the match and prepare for his exit in Ottawa. As history will forever recall, Bret lost the belt. Even though he never submitted to the Sharpshooter move of Shawn Michaels, referee Earl Hebner signalled the timekeeper to ring the bell. McMahon, who had been standing nearby, shouted: "Ring the bell, ring the bell." Bret couldn't believe what had happened and spat on him in disgust.

In a private conversation between the two earlier in the evening, McMahon and Bret discussed the outcome of the match. Bret proposed to McMahon that Michaels put Bret in the Sharpshooter — Bret would then reverse it, followed by a run-in of the Hart Foundation from the back, which would produce an automatic disqualification.

Bret had been wearing a hidden recording wire throughout the year of the documentary's filming and had the electronic device on during this key conversation with McMahon. As portrayed in the documentary, McMahon's recorded response to Bret's proposed outcome of the match was "to me that sounds great."

Dejected and disillusioned, Bret attempted to talk to McMahon, but the WWF owner had locked himself in his office. After urging from some of the wrestlers, McMahon left his room and headed into the dressing room where Bret was changing. Accompanied by six road agents, who were former wrestlers, and his son, Shane, McMahon barged into Bret's dressing room. He told McMahon to leave. When McMahon proceeded to move forward, Bret punched him in the jaw and knocked him out. Bret called it a "Stu Hart judgement call."

Pro Wrestling Almanac described the breakup as the top news story of 1997. "When the history of the war between the WWF and WCW is examined, this will surely be listed as one of the turning points. If you flesh out all the innuendo and bitterness, one sad fact remains: a 14-year relationship was left tattered, torn and perhaps beyond repair in a mire of deception and misunderstanding."

In his autobiography, Mick Foley (aka Mankind, Dude Love, Cactus Jack), wrote: "No one will ever forget the Survivor Series of November, 1997. It was without a doubt the most controversial night in the history of the business, the ramifications of which are still being felt today." He said that the backstage area was in a state of shock after Bret was swerved out of the title. "I was really upset by what I had just seen," Foley wrote. "You just don't do that to a guy like Bret Hart, is all I could say for minutes, as I repeated it over and

Bret squares off against Diamond Dallas Page.

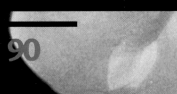

Bret finished Sting off with a baseball bat
in 1998 at Halloween Havoc in Las Vegas
at the MGM Grand Hotel.

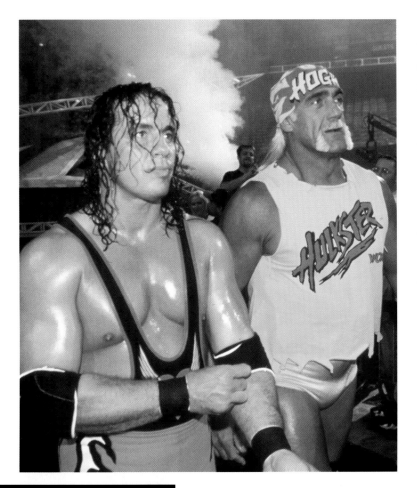

Bret and Hulk Hogan combine forces in a winning tag team match.

over." Foley almost quit the WWF as a protest to what happened. He did not wrestle the following night in Ottawa, but eventually rethought his decision and returned to the circuit because of financial reasons.

Dave Meltzer, the editor of the highly respected *Wrestling Observer*, wrote the Survivor Series finish will go down as "the most famous ending of a match in North American history. Bret Hart is among the leading candidates to be the pro wrestler of this decade. He's one of the best in-ring performers of this generation."

Bret had quit the WWF for good, vowing never to return to the company.

"If I can sum up myself, I think I was like Tom Hanks' character in *Saving Private Ryan*," Bret says. "I was sort of there for everybody all the years I was in the WWF. I was always the shoulder to lean on or the one to come to for advice. I think more and more I look back at all these different wrestlers over the years and I often gave them good advice and sound advice when they really needed it. I think a lot of them know what I did for that company and how I handled and conducted myself. I was definitely a team guy."

Bret had serious concerns about joining the WCW. During his WWF tenure, he was a proud company man. Hogan and Flair welcomed Bret with open arms to the WCW. Bret debuted at Starcade in Washington, D.C. in December, 1997 as a guest referee in a match between Larry Zbyszko and Bischoff, who was part of Hogan's nWo (New World Order) gang. Bret helped Zbyszko win and became a baby-face in the process. Bret won the U.S. Heavyweight title four times before he won the World Heavyweight title in Toronto on November 21, 1999.

Bret enters the arena at Halloween Havoc pay-per-view event in Vegas, October, 1998, ready for his match against Sting.

"WE WANT BRET."

NIGHTS TO REMEMBER

On March 29, 1999, wrestling fans filtered through the doors of the spanking-new Air Canada Centre in Toronto to witness history. The WCW had come to Canada for its first-ever Nitro broadcast. More important from a Canadian perspective, it marked Bret's inaugural show in his homeland with his new organization.

Well before the bell sounded for the opening match, the capacity crowd started shouting, "We want Bret, we want Bret." A slew of signs signified the fans' support for Bret. A sampling of the posters included: "Welcome Home, Bret"; "Hitman 4 Life"; "Bret Hart For Prime Minister." ■

Bret enters the Air Canada Centre, March 29, 1999, for the first Nitro event in Canada, wearing his Hitmen Sweater.

The noise level soared when the giant screen high above the ring showed a clip from the previous Nitro show in which Bret verbally challenged Goldberg, the former professional football player who had become the fastest rising star in the WCW.

"I could beat you and you'll be sorry you ever stepped into the ring with me," Bret said.

Like throwing wood into a raging fire, it further stoked the mounting excitement for The Hitman.

Midway into the card, Bret emerged from backstage and walked toward the ring, wearing a Calgary Hitmen jersey, while the fans collectively rose and gave him a hearty welcome. Bret took the microphone and did an emotional rendition of O Canada, saying the words slowly instead of singing. He touched a patriotic nerve in everyone, practically bringing the crowd and himself to tears. He talked about his love for Canada and how he had come to the WCW to make a reputation, not lose it, part of a retirement angle which had been discussed earlier in the day with Bischoff amid mounting rumours Bret planned to quit the WCW.

Bret verbally challenged Goldberg, the former professional football player who had become the fastest rising star in the WCW.

Bret then stripped off his jersey, revealing a Maple Leafs' jersey with the number of his friend Tie Domi, the team's rugged forward. It generated an even larger applause, but Goldberg tried to steal the moment when he rushed into the ring and rammed his bald head into Bret's breadbasket. The two wrestlers fell to the mat and laid there for what seemed like an eternity.

Slowly, Bret rose ahead of Goldberg and pinned him, much to the fans' delight. He then peeled off his jersey and revealed a metal breastplate strapped to his chest, which explained why Goldberg dropped to the mat upon contact.

To further add to the show, Bret grabbed the microphone and announced he was quitting the WCW and stormed off to the dressing room. Bret gave his fans a night to remember with some drama drenched in patriotism and intrigue.

"The whole thing was pretty cool," Bret says. "I thought this might be the only chance I ever got to steal the show and I wanted to steal it and give it to this crowd that had bought these tickets and had come to support me and defend me after what happened in Montreal. I was trying to sort of thank them and say something to the wrestling audience. You just never know when it will be all over and I always wanted to leave on a good note. That was a good note. There was a strong desire for me to walk away from wrestling for real when that show was over".

To further add to the show, Bret grabbed the microphone and announced he was quitting the WCW and stormed off to the dressing room. **Bret gave his fans a night to remember with** some drama drenched **in patriotism and intrigue.**

Bret beats Goldberg
with brains over brawn.

Goldberg runs into a dead-end in the Nitro confrontation with Bret a the Air Canada Centre in March 1999.

On November 21, almost eight months after the Nitro show, WCW returned to Toronto for its Mayhem pay-per-view event at the Air Canada Centre. Once again, much of the spotlight centered on Bret. He had advanced to the semi-finals of a tournament that began a month before to decide the Heavyweight champion. Bret would face Sting in one semi-final, while Chris Benoit would battle Jeff Jarrett in the other. The card attracted an audience of many Bret Hart fans, including a group of about 10 sitting in the first row near the ring wearing Calgary Hitmen jerseys.

Among the many signs was one — "Do It For Owen" — that was particularly touching. Owen's death earlier in the year had been felt by the entire wrestling world, which shared in the grief of the Hart family. Back in July, Bret appeared on a Nitro show from Atlanta and talked about the loss of his brother and how he was unsure about his future. Indeed, at that point Bret had no idea if he would ever wrestle again, but in the ensuing months he found the courage and strength to return.

You could almost feel a sense of anticipation throughout the arena that this was Bret's night to become the WCW's next Heavyweight champion. The crowd applauded warmly and loudly when Bret's wife, Julie, and the couple's four children — Jade, Dallas, Alexandra and Blade — took their seats about 10 rows from the ring.

Benoit won his match by smashing Jarrett over the head with his guitar and pinning him.

Bret appeared for his match against Sting wearing a Team Canada jersey with the number 99 of legendary superstar Wayne Gretzky, who was in town to be inducted into the Hockey Hall of Fame the next night. Wayne and Bret had become good friends over the years and had recently filmed a TV commercial in which The Great One wrestled The Excellence Of Execution.

Bret appeared for his match against Sting wearing a Team Canada jersey with the number 99 of legendary superstar Wayne Gretzky, who was in town to be inducted into the Hockey Hall of Fame the next night.

Sting and Bret stood eye-to-eye and then pushed one another, revving up the crowd in the process. The two stars squared off in a match that started out as a slugfest and carried over to the broadcast table.

Suddenly, The Total Package (the wrestler formerly known as Lex Luger) emerged and struck Sting in the knee with a bat. He then turned on Bret, who took away the bat and put him into the Sharpshooter. The Total Package screamed and pleaded with Bret to stop, which he did. Then Bret turned to the referee and pleaded with him not to disqualify Sting because he didn't want to win that way. The referee agreed and the match continued.

Sting appeared to be headed for the win when he put Bret in the Scorpion Deathlock. Bret reversed it and put the Sharpshooter on Sting, who tapped out. When Bret left the ring, Sting called him back to shake hands.

The all-Canadian final would pit two friends from Calgary. Many people considered Benoit the heir apparent to Bret because of his technical ability. The two had squared off in an historical match on Oct. 4 on a Nitro card at Kemper Arena in Kansas City. Anyone among the millions who watched the match in person or on TV would certainly agree it was one for the ages. It was in the same arena earlier in the year on May 23 that Owen plummetted to his premature death in a WWF pay-per-view event. WCW management told Bret he could skip the Nitro card at Kemper Arena, but he wanted to wrestle as a tribute to Owen. Bret and Chris, a longtime family friend who had learned the fundamentals of wrestling in the Dungeon, squared off in a 30-minute

"I wasn't really worried about winning or losing. I just wanted to be able to look at myself in the mirror and know that Owen would have been proud and I wanted the same for Chris Benoit. I could feel Owen watching -- as if he'd pulled up a chair, like a fan, eager to see something special from me and Chris."

match featuring technical and scientific skills. When it ended with Bret winning, he paid homage to Owen by saluting the sky. Later that week in his *Calgary Sun* column, Bret wrote: "I wasn't really worried about winning or losing. I just wanted to be able to look at myself in the mirror and know that Owen would have been proud and I wanted the same for Chris Benoit. I could feel Owen watching — as if he'd pulled up a chair, like a fan, eager to see something special from me and Chris. Something we all hadn't seen on TV for too long a time. 'Dungeon' wrestling. A straightforward, shoot-from-the-hip, wrestling match. Pro wrestling in its purest form, just two people telling a story with their bodies. Artistry at its best."

Now, some seven weeks later, Bret and Chris would square off once again. Both cut separate promos backstage, acknowledging their respect for one another but vowing not to let that get in the way of winning the belt.

Before the match began, the two shook hands and then engaged in a series of reversals and moves that glorified the art of wrestling. Bret had Benoit in the Sharpshooter, but the Canadian Crippler squirmed out of it and put The Crippler Crossface on the Hitman. Bret worked his way to the ropes, which forced Benoit to break the hold. The two then shook hands in appreciation of each other's skills.

The match took a different twist when Dean Malenko, wearing a Team Canada jersey and the red and white Canadian colors on his face, marched toward the ring with a Canadian flag. This tied in with the story line earlier in the card in which a fan wearing similar colors and seated near the ring, attacked Malenko during the mixed tag-team elimination between The Revolution and The Filthy Animals. The fan was ejected by security, but it was all contrived. Malenko began attacking Benoit with the flag, but Bret intervened and security removed Malenko.

The match began again and after Benoit delivered a diving headbutt, The Outsiders — Scott Hall and Kevin Nash — pulled referee Charles Robinson out of the ring and knocked him out. The Outsiders then entered the ring and Hall attacked Benoit with a chair and Nash moved in on Bret. Goldberg rushed in from the back and chased away Hall and Nash.

In the 17th minute of the historic match, The Canadian Crippler had Bret in the Crippler Crossface. Chris appeared headed for the coveted belt, but Bret elbowed his way out of the hold and put Benoit in the Sharpshooter and he tapped out.

Bret was declared the winner and handed the championship belt. He joined Randy Savage, Hulk Hogan, Ric Flair and Kevin Nash as the only winners of the Heavyweight belt in both the WWF and WCW. Julie and three of the four children joined Bret in the ring, along with Wayne Gretzky's three children — Paulina, Trevor and Ty — and a family friend. Benoit came over and shook hands with Bret, who draped the belt around Blade's shoulders. Bret was then handed a Canadian flag, which he unfurled and proudly paraded around the ring, while the crowd cheered madly.

This was a marked contrast to the sad ending almost two years before when Bret found himself humiliated in front of his family, friends and myriad of fans around the world. Wrestling fans rejoiced in Bret's latest championship, as evidenced by some of these messages on his website: "Respect shown among two athletes was wonderful, something we don't get to see too often," wrote one fan. "Finally a wrong was made right and Bret won the belt in Canada." Another one summed it up perfectly: "To me, Bret Hart is still the WWF champ because he never lost to Shawn in Montreal and now he is the undisputed WCW Heavyweight champ." ❦

A great moment for Bret — one of the memorable highlights of his career winning the WCW World Heavyweight Champion Title.

BRET HART'S TITLE REIGNS (... SO FAR)

WWF WORLD HEAVYWEIGHT TITLE

1 Defeated Ric Flair in Saskatoon, Saskatchewan, on October 12, 1992. Lost it to Yokozuna in Las Vegas, Nevada on April 4, 1993.

2 Defeated Yokozuna in New York, New York, on March 20, 1994. Lost it to Bob Backland in San Antonio, Texas on November 23, 1994.

3 Defeated Diesel (Kevin Nash) in Landover, Maryland on November 19, 1995. Lost it to Shawn Michaels in Anaheim, California on March 31, 1996.

4 Defeated The Undertaker, Stone Cold Steve Austin and Vader during a Four Corners Elimination bout in Chattanooga, Tennessee on February 16, 1997. Lost it to Psycho Sid (Sid Vicious, Sid Justice) on February 17, 1997.

5 Defeated The Undertaker in East Rutherford, New Jersey, on August 3, 1997. Lost it to Shawn Michaels in Montreal, Quebec on November 9, 1997 when Vince McMahon called for the bell in Bret's last match for the WWF and awarded the title to Michaels.

WWF INTERCONTINENTAL HEAVYWEIGHT TITLE

1 Defeated Mr. Perfect (Curt Hennig) in Madison Square Garden in New York on August 26, 1991. Lost it to The Mountie (Jacques Rougeau) in Springfield, Maryland on January 17, 1992.

2 Defeated Roddy Piper in Indianapolis, Indiana on April 5, 1992. Lost it to The British Bulldog (Davey Boy Smith) in London, England on August 29, 1992.

WWF WORLD TAG TEAM TITLES

1 With Jim Neidhart defeated the British Bulldogs in Tampa, Florida on January 26, 1987. Lost the title to Strike Force (Rick Martel and Tito Santana) in Syracuse, New York on October 27, 1987.

2 With Jim Neidhart defeated Demolition (Crush and Smash) in Philadelphia, Pennsylvania on August 27, 1990. Lost the title to the Nasty Boys (Brian Knobs and Jerry Sags) in Los Angeles, California on March 24, 1991.

WCW UNITED STATES HEAVYWEIGHT TITLE

1 Defeated Diamond Dallas Page in Salt Lake City, Utah, on July 20, 1998. Lost it to Lex Luger in Rapid City, South Dakota on August 10, 1998.

2 Defeated Lex Luger in Fargo, North Dakota on August 13, 1998. Lost it to Diamond Dallas Page in Phoenix, Arizona on October 20, 1998.

3 Defeated Diamond Dallas Page in Chattanooga, Tennessee on November 30, 1998. Lost it to Roddy Piper in Buffalo, New York, on February 8, 1999.

4 Defeated Bill Goldberg in Phoenix, Arizona on October 25, 1999 and then vacated the title.

STAMPEDE WRESTLING — NORTH AMERICAN HEAVYWEIGHT TITLE

1 Defeated Leo Burke in 1980. Lost it to Leo Burke in 1980.

2 Defeated Leo Burke in May of 1980. Lost it to Duke Myers in 1980.

3 Defeated Duke Myers in 1980. Lost it to David Shults in 1981.

4 Defeated Leo Burke on June 26, 1982. Lost it to Bad News Allen on September 3, 1982.

5 Defeated Bad News Allen on October 17, 1982. Lost it to Leo Burke on January 14, 1983.

6 Defeated Leo Burke in Regina, Saskatchewan on May 3, 1983. Lost it to Bad News Allen in June, 1983.

STAMPEDE WRESTLING — INTERNATIONAL TAG TEAM TITLE

1 With Keith Hart defeated Raul and Fidel Castillo in December, 1978. Lost the titles to Mr. Hito and Mr. Sakurada in 1979.

2 With Keith Hart defeated Mr. Hito and Mr. Sakurada in 1979. Lost the titles to The Dynamite Kid and The Loch Ness Monster in 1980.

3 With Keith Hart defeated The Dynamite Kid and The Loch Ness Monster in 1980. Lost the titles to The Dynamite Kid and Kasavudu in 1980.

4 With Keith Hart defeated the Dynamite Kid and Kasavudu in 1980. Lost the titles to Kasavudu and Mr. Sakurada in 1980.

5 With Leo Burke: defeated Duke Myers and The Dynamite Kid on November 19, 1982. Lost the titles to Duke Myers and Kerry Brown, on December 8, 1982.

BRITISH COMMONWEALTH MID-HEAVYWEIGHT TITLE

1 Defeated Norman Frederick Charles III in 1978. Lost the title to The Dynamite Kid in 1978.

2 Defeated the Dynamite Kid in 1979. Lost the title to The Dynamite Kid in 1979.

WCW WORLD HEAVYWEIGHT CHAMPION TITLEBELT

**Defeats Chris Benoit at
Air Canada Centre, November 21, 1999**

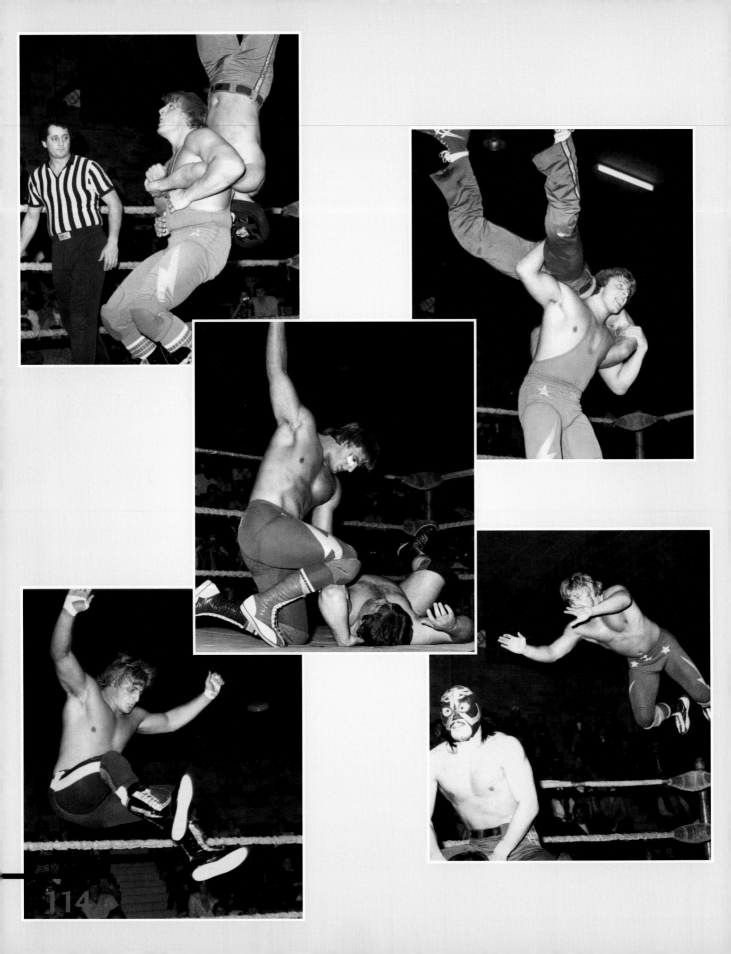

REFLECTIONS OF A
BIG BROTHER

by Bret Hart

"You were a great wrestler from start to finish and millions of your fans around the world will never let that be forgotten."

"My mother and father, I know what he meant to you, to all of us Harts, and I hope in our sadness, we can find some way to overcome this tragedy and move on again."

I just can't believe it.

My brother Owen has been taken away from me. He was such a wonderful human and I will miss him so much. I've tried and tried to sum up into words what he meant to me. What he meant to all of us who loved him.

It seems everyone knows by now what a great husband, father, son and brother he was.

"I know you were proud of your accomplishments, as I was."

He was, without a doubt, the finest family man that I ever knew.

His life was centered around his wife, Martha, his one and only childhood sweetheart, and his two beautiful children, Oje and Athena.

So many times I remember he sprinted from the door of the plane, his two carry-on bags in each hand, at a full run, worn out and weary, just to clear customs, through the sliding doors, to their outstretched arms.

A man with no vices. None.

And oh, how he loved them all!

I don't believe anyone knew Owen as well as me, except Martha.

I recall, so often, in airports, hotel rooms, dressing rooms, long drives on endless highways, his only dream was to come home to his wife and his two children.

He almost made it, only days before moving into their dream home.

He worked so hard for that dream. It's all so unfair, an exhausting argument with God.

A long and sad meditation on fate and purpose and love.

I'm so sorry, Martha. You and he deserved so much to have all your dreams come true.

As your brother, if you can hear me, and I know you can, you would be very proud of her. I understand, even more so than before, why you fell in love with this girl and why you loved her so much.

"Owen, I loved wrestling with you. You were a great wrestler from start to finish and millions of your fans all around the world will never let that be forgotten."

As your brother, I promise to watch over Athena and Oje. To be there for them.

To try my best to make up for your absence. To tell them about you and to never let them wonder what you were like. To help Martha forever and to ensure what you wanted most: that Oje and Athena are raised with respect and love and that they'll be guided by your spirit to have integrity and conscience. That they will make you proud.

Martha wouldn't have it any other way.

Neither will I.

My mother and father, I know what he meant to you, to all of us Harts, and I hope in our sadness, we can find some way to overcome this tragedy and move on again.

The Harts are loved and admired for our strength.

This will be a true test.

We all have many wonderful and beautiful thoughts and memories of Owen. I wouldn't know where to start. I can't.

I've concluded that we can only hold on to all those memories and like our lost brother, Dean, we will laugh and smile and talk endlessly of how you made this world a better place.

Owen, you were the funniest person I knew. I thank you for that.

I will smile to myself forever at all the funny things you did.

A prankster?

Nobody but all of us who knew you will ever understand how hilarious it was to be around you.

Prank me anytime, Owen, I'll be waiting for your call.

"I don't believe anyone knew Owen as well as me, except Martha."

You were a great man who never, ever lost the heart of a child.

I will hold dear my memories of all the places, distant lands and people we saw together.

The sunset in Guam. The breathtaking beauty of Cape Town, South Africa. Our hell ride to the Taj Mahal in India. The serenity and beauty of the Hong Kong skyline. The harsh realities of Hiroshima and Auschwitz, where we paid our silent respect, and maybe more importantly our trip to Jerusalem, the ceaseless wonder.

For, like Jesus nailed to the cross, to a grid of paradoxes, you balanced yourself between the torment of not knowing your mission and the joy you took in carrying it out.

Owen, you have all the answers now. I remember always being your protector. Looking out for you.

I feel my heartache and my eyes begin to sting when I think: why wasn't I there to protect you in the Kemper Arena in Kansas City.

To question if this was really necessary . . . .

Owen, I loved wrestling with you.

You were a great wrestler from start to finish and millions of your fans all around the world will never let that be forgotten.

Maybe it's not important, almost kind of meaningless, but I know you were proud of your accomplishments, as I was, and you were one of the greatest athletes to ever set foot in a wrestling ring.

Everyone has a song in their heart.

My families have always been in professional wrestling.

The hardest aspect of it was always the never-ending loneliness.

In reflection of that, both you and I understood from the very start that we were singing a very sad song.

For no matter what anyone ever thinks, Owen, yours will always be the most beautiful song I've ever heard.

I'm lonely for you already.

The world loved you very much and we will all miss you for a very long time.

**Your loving brother,
Bret**

"Reproduced from Bret Hart's column in the *Calgary Sun*, May 31, 1999 for all his fans to see and read again because the words he wrote when Owen died were raw and true."

Bret and Owen ham it up during the "Honey I
Shrunk the Kids" episode filmed in October 1998.

"The world loved you very much and we will all miss you for a very long time."

Owen Hart
1965 – 1999

Perry Lefko

Perry Lefko has been reporting on sports for the Toronto Sun since 1985. He has written two previous books: The Greatest Show on Turf, A History of the Breeders' Cup, and Flutie, the autobiography of Doug Flutie. Perry lives in Mississauga, Ontario, Canada with his wife, Jane, and son, Ben, and daughter, Shayna, who collectively are known as the Lefko Foundation and are avid wrestling fans.

Photo Credits

- Cover, p. 64 — **Mark Mennie**
- p. 2, 14, 20 (all), 24, 25, 44, 56, 57, 58, 59, 60, 61, 70, 71, 76, 77, 78, 80, 84, 88, 89, 90, 92, 93 (all), 95, 96 (3 small), 97 (all), 99, 100-101, 102, 103 (all), 104 (all, 105 (all), 106 (all), 107, 113, 127, — **Rik Fedyck**
- p. 8 —**Roddy Piper**
- p. 10, 18, 36 (all), 37, 38, 39 (all), 42, 45, 46 (all), 47, 48 (all), 49, 50, 51, 54, 111, 114 (all), 118 — **Stampede Wrestling**
- p. 11, 15, 31, 33, 34, 35, 62, 66, 85, 86, 108, 116, 119, 121, 123, 124-125 — **Calgary Sun**
- p. 17, 23, 81 — **Chris Large**
- p. 19 — **Glen Reichwein**
- p. 20-21, 87 — **Balmur Entertainment**
- p. 22 (Bret with Gretzky, Bret with Stern), 83 — **Teri Tkachuk**
- p. 26, 27, 28, 40, 41, 117 — **Bret & Hart Family**
- p. 30 — **Jeff McIntosh**
- p. 52, 55, 63, 67, 73, 74, 75, 82, 91 — **WCW**
- p. 126 — **unknown fan**
- p. 13, 69, 96, 97 — **Toronto Sun**